Becoming Powerful

HOW TO GET THINGS DONE IN
THE KINGDOM OF GOD

JOHN BRADBURY

ISBN: 1535328592

ISBN-13: 978-1535328593

CONTENTS

	PREFACE	7
1	OFFICERS OF THE COURT	13
2	THE RENEWED MIND	25
3	NOTHING SHALL BE IMPOSSIBLE	43
4	YOU SHALL RECEIVE POWER	61
5	THERE'S MORE!	73
6	HOSTING HIS PRESENCE	85
7	LOVE IS...	101
8	GROWING IN LOVE	113
9	THE GREENHOUSE EFFECT	123

PREFACE

FAITH, HOPE & LOVE

Seven years. I spent seven years studying and meditating on one chapter of the bible. The chapter is John 14 and there is so much depth in the word of God you could probably spend an entire lifetime on that chapter and still get new revelation from it. What happens when you spend a lot of time in one passage is, as Allen Hood says, "the fog begins to lift." That means the details that seem unclear begin to sharpen and you start to see the whole picture in a clearer way. Slowly, three concepts began to emerge as central to the gospel and I began to see them throughout the scriptures - believe, love and obey.

[Jhn 14:11-21 NKJV] 11 "Believe Me that I [am] in the Father and the Father in Me, or else believe Me for the sake of the works themselves. 12 "Most assuredly, I say to you, he who believes in Me, the works that I do he will do also; and greater [works] than these he will do, because I go to My Father. 13 "And whatever you ask in My name, that I will do, that the Father may be glorified in the Son. 14 "If you ask anything in My name, I will do [it]. 15 "If you love Me, keep My commandments. 16 "And I will pray the Father, and He will give you another Helper, that He may abide with you forever-- 17 "the Spirit of truth, whom the world cannot receive, because it neither sees Him nor knows Him; but you know Him, for He dwells with you and will be in you. 18 "I will not leave you orphans; I will come to you. 19 "A little while longer and the world will see Me no more, but you will see Me. Because I live, you will live also. 20 "At that day you will know that I [am] in My Father, and you in Me, and I in you. 21 "He who has My commandments and keeps them, it is he who loves Me. And he who loves Me will be loved by My Father, and I will love him and manifest Myself to him."

Believing, loving and obeying are the catalysts that produce greater works, answered prayer, the outpouring of the Spirit, our identity in Christ, and the release of His manifest presence. Wow! So simple and so powerful, but not often understood or practiced. Believing, or faith, has to do with our confidence in who Jesus is, what He says, and how He did what He did. Love has to do with our personal relationship and history with God. It is communion and worship and fellowship with His heart and it always moves us toward obedience. When we love, then we obey, and that releases the presence of the Holy Spirit and encounters with the manifest presence of God. Encounters with God take us to new levels of revelation, understanding, and breakthrough and we start the whole process over at a new level of maturity and closeness to the heart of God.

This is the maturing process of the Christian life. This is how our inner man becomes stronger and grows into who we are supposed to be. We relate to God by believing in Him, loving Him, and obeying Him and He responds and good things happen inside of us.

However, the Christian life is not only about maturity and personal growth, it is also about releasing the power of the kingdom into the lives of others. In 1 Corinthians 12-14 Paul describes how we relate to each other, the spiritual realm, and how we release the power of God into the lives of people. He explains the importance of spiritual gifts and love and how they relate to each other. Right in the middle of this profound passage he summarises with this verse:

[1Co 13:13 NKJV] 13 And now abide faith, hope, love, these three; but the greatest of these [is] love.

Faith, hope and love are not just character qualities that we develop, they are the means by which we release heaven to earth. They are the channels through which the power of the kingdom flows into the lives of others.

Faith is the believing that we mentioned from John 14. We believe and power is released in us and through us. Hope is the atmosphere of the manifest presence; it is the anointing of the Spirit. Hope is the dimension where anything is possible inside our hearts or through our lives. It is the the release of the Holy Spirit and the manifest presence of John 14. Love is the most powerful force in the universe. It is the way He feels, why He gives, and the essence of the gospel. Love is the means and the end, the reason why we are brought into a position of closeness as sons of God and as the bride of Christ.

In this book we are going to explore these three fundamental aspects of the kingdom: faith, hope and love. So many believers are struggling to just survive. They do not know what the will of God is for their life or how to get there. They need fathers and mothers who will go deep into the heart of God and make a way for them to follow. Will you be one? Are you satisfied with having just enough for yourself, or will you become one who is a resource for others? If so, read on to discover how we can move from survivors to powerful believers.

Becoming Powerful is broken up into three sections with three chapters in each section. In each section there is a chapter discovering what faith, hope and love is, how we grow in them in our inner man, and how we use them to release the power of God into the lives of others. My prayer for you as you read this book is from Ephesians 1:

[Eph 1:16-19 NKJV] 16 do not cease to give thanks for you, making mention of you in my prayers: 17 that the God of our Lord Jesus Christ, the Father of glory, may give to you the spirit of wisdom and revelation in the knowledge of Him, 18 the eyes of your understanding being enlightened; that you may know what is the hope of His calling, what are the riches of the glory of His inheritance in the saints, 19 and what [is] the exceeding greatness of His power toward us who believe, according to the working of His mighty power

May you become powerful inside and out as the revelation of the kingdom expands in your heart and mind.

FAITH

CHAPTER 1

OFFICERS OF THE COURT

[Eph 1:16-23 NKJV] 16 do not cease to give thanks for you, making mention of you in my prayers: 17 that the God of our Lord Jesus Christ, the Father of glory, may give to you the spirit of wisdom and revelation in the knowledge of Him, 18 the eyes of your understanding being enlightened; that you may know what is the hope of His calling, what are the riches of the glory of His inheritance in the saints, 19 and what [is] the exceeding greatness of His power toward us who believe, according to the working of His mighty power 20 which He worked in Christ when He raised Him from the dead and seated [Him] at His right hand in the heavenly [places],

21 far above all principality and power and might and dominion, and every name that is named, not only in this age but also in that which is to come. 22 And He put all [things] under His feet, and gave Him [to be] head over all [things] to the church, 23 which is His body, the fullness of Him who fills all in all.

[Eph 2:1-6 NKJV] 1 And you [He made alive], who were dead in trespasses and sins, 2 in which you once walked according to the course of this world, according to the prince of the power of the air, the spirit who now works in the sons of disobedience, 3 among whom also we all once conducted ourselves in the lusts of our flesh, fulfilling the desires of the flesh and of the mind, and were by nature children of wrath, just as the others. 4 But God, who is rich in mercy, because of His great love with which He loved us, 5 even when we were dead in trespasses, made us alive together with Christ (by grace you have been saved), 6 and raised [us] up together, and made [us] sit together in the heavenly [places] in Christ Jesus

Imagine you lived in a country ruled by an all powerful and loving king. He has the authority of the president, the congress, and the supreme court all rolled into one. He makes the laws, interprets and applies the laws, and makes all the judgments on who is right and wrong. The military is led by Him and completely loyal to Him. Good is the only way to describe His character, and everything He says and does is loving, kind, and just.

In the kingdom of God that is how it is, and right now every person who has the Spirit of God in them lives in that kingdom. When you believed in Jesus as savior and lord, you became a part of a family business called the kingdom of God. Right now you are seated in heaven as a son of God with both the authority and the inheritance that sons have. You have legal access to every promise God ever made and every gift He ever gave.

God's heart and His will was demonstrated by Jesus, and His desire is that every person on earth have a relationship with Him and access to heaven through His Spirit. His will, or you could say His law, is that all the works of the devil be destroyed and that every person be free to voluntarily choose Him. So why is that not fully happening? The answer is simple; faith is required to take what is legally available to us and provide access to it on the earth.

[Eph 3:10-12 NKJV] 10 to the intent that now the manifold wisdom of God might be made known by the church to the principalities and powers in the heavenly [places], 11 according to the eternal purpose which He accomplished in Christ Jesus our Lord, 12 in whom we have boldness and access with confidence through faith in Him.

When we believe we can take the things that are legally ours and make them reality. The process by which that happens is called revelation and it results in us having our minds renewed.

[Rom 12:2 NKJV] 2 And do not be conformed to this world, but be transformed by the renewing of your mind, that you may prove what [is] that good and acceptable and perfect will of God.

REVELATION BASED AUTHORITY

Here is how it works. When we give our hearts to Jesus, we get access to what He has access to. Relationship with the Father, the anointing of the Spirit, authority over the devil, an eternal inheritance that includes a new body and living forever with Him, healing for our bodies and souls, wisdom, forgiveness, prosperity, peace and joy are all ours. The list could go on and on, but you get the point. Jesus' death and resurrection gave us legal access to all of those things for both ourselves and those we love. But in order to access them we have to first know that they are available and then believe that we can have them now.

As we saw in Ephesians, it is revelation, understanding, and wisdom that show us what our position and inheritance is. Gradually the Holy Spirit shows us what Jesus did for us and we begin to think like a son of God and our mind gets renewed. Technically, everything Jesus bought and paid for is ours right now, but we can not prove or demonstrate that it is ours until our mind is renewed. All of this process requires that we have an intimate relationship with the Spirit of God so that we can hear when He tells us the truth of who God is, what He is like, what He said, what His will is, and who we are to Him.

[Rom 10:17 NKJV] 17 So then faith [comes] by hearing, and hearing by the word of God.

We get to know God and how He talks through the Bible. The written scriptures are such a beautiful and amazing gift from God. We can see clearly how God talks, the way He relates to people, and His general will for humanity in the scriptures. But the Bible by itself does not provide all we need to access and prove the will of God for us personally. We need a real and living relationship with the Spirit of God so that we can hear the specifics He wants to tell us now so that we can believe and demonstrate it. The Bible gives us what God said and the Spirit gives us what He is saying.

PUBLIC SERVANTS

Now let's go back to our analogy. If God is the good King in the kingdom and we know what His will is, then we become officers of the court that enforce His rule in our spheres of influence. We are the police officer, the district attorney, or the district judge that takes the will of God and enforces, proves, and demonstrates it. When we both understand and submit to the authority of the Lordship of Jesus we have authority to do His will. Just because God wills something does not mean that it is automatically done; it has to be enforced. Remember the gospel story where the centurion asked Jesus to heal his servant:

[Luk 7:8-9 NKJV] 8 "For I also am a man placed under authority, having soldiers under me. And I say to one, 'Go,' and he goes; and to another, 'Come,' and he comes; and to my servant, 'Do this,' and he does [it]." 9 When Jesus heard these things, He marveled at him, and turned around and said to the crowd that followed Him, "I say to you, I have not found such great faith, not even in Israel!"

The centurion understood that Jesus had placed Himself under God's authority and therefore was in a position to command God's will to be done in the situation. Jesus knew that this understanding was the key to getting things done in the kingdom, and He called it great faith. When we understand the heart of the King and get revelation of what His will is in a situation we can position ourselves in our rightful place as public servants under the King and carry out His will for the sake of the kingdom.

WHAT IS FAITH?

So what is faith exactly? Hebrews 11 says that "Faith is the substance of things hoped for," but what does that mean? Faith is believing, but believing what?

First, faith is believing in who God is. As we learned earlier, faith comes by hearing or getting revelation from the Bible and the Spirit of God, and that requires a relationship. So the Holy Spirit reveals to us things about the Father and the Son and we begin to trust that they are true. We start to put confidence in the revelation we are hearing and begin to think, talk and act accordingly. Then He begins to reveal more and more of who He is and what He is like. Goodness and mercy, kindness and love, power and majesty get revealed to our hearts and we trust that He is who He said He is. The more we use the revelation we get, the more He adds to it. This is a never ending journey into the heart of God in which He continually expands our understanding and we respond with ever increasing trust in His impeccable character.

Next, faith is believing what God says. This is more than just trusting His character and heart, it is trusting His position of authority and power to speak and decree things into existence.

He created everything by speaking it into existence. His words are life, and they release the power and Spirit of God. He breathed into Adam's lungs and made him into a living being. God's words are the law of the land, the very reason why things exist. At the very heart of our relationship with God is communication: dreams, visions, impressions, scripture, pictures, feelings, words, and even His audible voice. He is an amazing communicator and we are His sheep who know His voice.

When He speaks it is not just revealing to us information about reality, it is actually creating reality. When we hear His voice we respond by changing the way we think, talk, and act. That is faith. Confidently trusting that what He says is not only true but creative power, and acting accordingly. Of course, we do not know everything He says or all of His will at once, but we continue to get more access based on how we used what He told us. Jesus said in Luke 6 that with the same measure we use it will be measured to us. In other words, if you believe and respond with a teaspoon of faith, then you get teaspoons of revelation. But if you believe and respond with dump truck loads of faith, then you get dump truck loads of revelation.

Lastly, faith is believing in the anointing that is on your life. We will talk about this more later in the book, but let's touch on it a little now. Love is what determines our sphere of influence.

We have no influence with someone we do not care about. When we love others, God responds by trusting us with delegated authority to help those people in some way. The same Holy Spirit who anointed Jesus comes upon us to empower us to minister to others. He anoints us with His power for a specific purpose and a specific group of people. Either through direct encounter or impartation, the Spirit comes upon us and trusts us to do for those people what Jesus did for His people.

Faith is believing that when you receive the anointing to do something, you have the same power Jesus has. Faith is acting like you are a public servant empowered from above to put the devil in his place and help God's people. Many people encounter the Holy Spirit in powerful ways, but continue to think they are the same powerless person as before. But faith believes, responds and acts like everything has changed because of the Holy Spirit. When God trusts us with His Spirit and His people, it is like Him giving us a uniform, badge, and gun and saying, "you are responsible for these people, keep them safe." We do not put our trust in ourselves, but in the anointing that covers and empowers us.

As we seek out and yield to the responsibility that the anointing requires, continue to grow in love, and believe that it is His Spirit on us that changes everything, He gives us more.

When we trust Him more He trusts us more, expanding both our sphere of influence and our power to make a difference.

Faith is trust, confidence and belief in who God is, what He says, and the anointing He trusts us with. Faith always comes from revelation, which results in our minds being renewed. Faith always results in a change of thinking, talking and action. To the degree we respond to Him, He continues to give us more and we grow in our relationship with Him and our boldness to act on His orders.

FAITH

CHAPTER 2

THE RENEWED MIND

[Rom 10:17 NKJV] 17 So then faith [comes] by hearing, and hearing by the word of God.

Faith is what draws things from one world into another. Good, powerful, helpful things exist in the kingdom of God, and faith takes them from that realm and imposes them on our current reality. Therefore, we want more faith, and we want to know how to use what we have. This chapter is about that very thing, how to increase your faith.

At the very core of the issue is communication. In order for your outward circumstances to start looking like the kingdom of Heaven, your internal reality has to look like it. In other words, if you are going to demonstrate and release wholeness into someone's life, it will only be released if you are whole inside. Peace inside releases peace outside. For example, Jesus was able to command a storm to stop because His internal reality was peace. This process whereby your inner man resembles the kingdom can only take place through communication between the two.

The Spirit of God comes into you and creates a link between you and the Father, between your inner man and heaven. When He speaks to you it is not just information, it is an encounter in which you are moved and changed by the grace transferred through His words. For this to happen on a regular basis, several things have to happen: you have to take time to listen, you have to know He is the one talking, you have to understand what He is saying, and you have to respond to what He is saying. When those things are in place, then the Christian life becomes a constant opportunity for inner transformation that results in outward power. Let's begin the process.

LAYING THE FOUNDATION

[Psa 1:1-3 NKJV] 1 Blessed [is] the man Who walks not in the counsel of the ungodly, Nor stands in the path of sinners, Nor sits in the seat of the scornful; 2 But his delight [is] in the law of the LORD, And in His law he meditates day and night. 3 He shall be like a tree Planted by the rivers of water, That brings forth its fruit in its season, Whose leaf also shall not wither; And whatever he does shall prosper.

[Psa 119:97 NKJV] 97 MEM. Oh, how I love Your law! It [is] my meditation all the day.

If hearing is the basis for faith, then the word of God is the basis for hearing. When we study the scripture, we learn how the Author talks and how He thinks. We read the Bible on a regular basis, we listen to it, memorize it, and meditate on it all the time. We study the language and the context to know not just what He said, but what He meant. Often we pray the verses, singing them into our spirits. We listen to preachers and teachers expound the word, and read what others have written about it.

Disciplines do not change our minds and hearts, encounters do. But purposely and practically immersing ourselves in the scriptures creates the environment for those encounters. As Jesus said in John 5:

[Jhn 5:38-40 NKJV] 38 "But you do not have His word abiding in you, because whom He sent, Him you do not believe. 39 "You search the Scriptures, for in them you think you have eternal life; and these are they which testify of Me. 40 "But you are not willing to come to Me that you may have life.

The scriptures themselves do not bring life, but if in our study of them we purposely discover Jesus, the living word, then we can use the Bible as a valuable tool in our relationship with Him. Our knowledge of the Bible is like the foundation we build our house on, the house being our living relationship with Jesus. It is not the house, but without it the house would be shaky.

I have never met or heard of anyone that has impacted the world for Christ that did not have a love for the scriptures. From the apostles of the early church through all of church history, it is difficult to identify even one who was making a difference that did not see the extreme value in the Bible. In our quest to know Him and make Him known we have to lay the foundation well, taking the whole of scripture and learning it with zeal. Never taking our favorite verses and twisting them to say what we want, but letting the entirety of the word taken in context shape the way we think and hearing what God wants to say to us.

SEEK HER AS SILVER

[Pro 2:1-6 NKJV] 1 My son, if you receive my words, And treasure my commands within you, 2 So that you incline your ear to wisdom, [And] apply your heart to understanding; 3 Yes, if you cry out for discernment, [And] lift up your voice for understanding, 4 If you seek her as silver, And search for her as [for] hidden treasures; 5 Then you will understand the fear of the LORD, And find the knowledge of God. 6 For the LORD gives wisdom; From His mouth [come] knowledge and understanding;

As the foundation is being laid of the knowledge of the word of God, we must not be satisfied with just information. Many of the deadest people I have met had a good base of knowledge of the Bible. Information does not bring life, but wisdom, understanding and revelation do. So what is the difference? One person is reading the Bible like a history book, or studying because of religious duty, while the other is being taught the scripture by the very same Holy Spirit who wrote it!

We have to treat the understanding of what God has said and is saying as the most valuable thing in our entire lives. It is literally more valuable than money, favor, influence, health or relationships because those are all byproducts of the central thing - wisdom. Like Solomon we must value wisdom, understanding and a hearing ear more than anything in life. Read the above passage from Proverbs 2 again and look at the action words used: receive, treasure, incline your ear, apply your heart, cry out, lift up your voice, seek and search. Do those words describe your devotional time?

If someone gave you a bag of jewels or a briefcase of cash, how would you treat it? Would you be careless and casual or would you be diligent and protective? If someone showed you one hundred million dollars and told you it was yours in a year if you finished a series of challenges, how hard would you try? Understanding the words, heart, and will of God is more valuable than that. It is priceless and can only be bought at one price - everything you've got. Only 100% will purchase this prize. Will you pay the price? Remember the parable of the treasure in the field in Matthew 13? It was only after he saw the value of the treasure and sold all he had that he could purchase it.

MY WORDS ABIDE IN YOU

[Jhn 15:7 NKJV] 7 "If you abide in Me, and My words abide in you, you will ask what you desire, and it shall be done for you.

The words of God are alive. They are not just alive metaphorically, meaning they are current, powerful, and meaningful. Of course His words are current, powerful and meaningful, but they are more than that. The words themselves are living and life giving substance that contain creative power in their DNA. Jesus said in John 6:

[Jhn 6:63 NKJV] 63 "It is the Spirit who gives life; the flesh profits nothing. The words that I speak to you are spirit, and [they] are life.

The words that He speaks do not just cause life, they are life. God does not just talk to pass the time or to have fun. Every time He speaks creative life and power are released.

In the analogy that Jesus used in John 15, He is the vine and we are the branches. He is the established source and we are the bearers of fruit. In this picture, His words are like the life giving sap that flows through Him into us bringing water and nutrients. We stay firmly established in our relationship and intimacy with Him, and His words are daily drawn into us bringing with them everything we need for a fruitful life.

Let's imagine another picture. A trusted and beloved family member is traveling from the Father to your city with purpose and power to accomplish something there. You hear that he is coming and make a room available to stay in your house as long as he needs. "Please come stay with me," you say and you make available to him anything in your house that he needs while he is there. That is the idea that is conveyed when Jesus talks about His word abiding in you. Every word He speaks is sent to accomplish something. You open your soul and receive it with joy and host it until it has done it's job. His words live in you, you feed them, host them, and transport them like that trusted family member.

We must value and honor each and every word God says to us no matter how it comes. Prophetic words or preaching, Bible study and reading, dreams, visions or impressions all must be welcomed in and celebrated. Through honor, the word is invited to abide in us as we abide in Him, creating the environment for fruit-filled prayers, families, ministries and lives.

SPIRITUALLY MINDED

[Rom 8:5-6 NKJV] 5 For those who live according to the flesh set their minds on the things of the flesh, but those [who live] according to the Spirit, the things of the Spirit. 6 For to be carnally minded [is] death, but to be spiritually minded [is] life and peace.

[1Co 14:1 NKJV] 1 Pursue love, and desire spiritual [gifts], but especially that you may prophesy.

[Col 3:2 NKJV] 2 Set your mind on things above, not on things on the earth.

Everyone talks not only in a certain language, but also from a certain perspective or culture. Sure, someone may speak multiple languages or even from more than one culture, but they still end up with a perspective from which they speak. God is no different. Obviously, God knows everything, created everything and can do anything. All languages and cultures originated from Him and He could make more if He wanted. My point is not to limit God, but to describe how He talks.

God the Father, Son and Holy Spirit exist in an environment very different than the one we are used to. Let's call it the culture of heaven. Since God breathed into Adam and created living human beings, God has been talking to us. His desire is clear and constant interaction with everyone of us, but that is not always possible. Every person has different levels of faith, different levels of intimacy with Him, and differing abilities to hear when He speaks. Some people have not yet been cleansed in the blood of Jesus and brought into relationship with God. Others do not even know or believe that He speaks to us anymore. Still others are listening but need to grow in their understanding and revelation.

[Num 12:6-8 NKJV] 6 Then He said, "Hear now My words: If there is a prophet among you, [I], the LORD, make Myself known to him in a vision; I speak to him in a dream. 7 Not so with My servant Moses; He [is] faithful in all My house. 8 I speak with him face to face, Even plainly, and not in dark sayings; And he sees the form of the LORD. Why then were you not afraid To speak against My servant Moses?"

So how does God talk? He is so personal and powerful that He often speaks in a language that is unique to us. However, the methods by which He speaks and the culture from which He speaks remain the same. Remember that He is God; He does not have to change for us, we have to change for Him. We have to do what the scriptures say: set our mind on the things of the Spirit, renew our minds, and desire the spiritual. Jesus came and became a part of our culture so that we can go and become a part of His. If we can not hear and understand what He is saying, the problem is not on His end but ours. We must take the time and effort to learn His culture and language. Do not assume that He is not speaking because you do not hear or understand, but take the time to tune your ears to the way He speaks.

Let's look at some of the ways God speaks to us so we can grow in our understanding.

THE BIBLE: while we are reading, studying, or meditating, He "highlights" a verse, phrase or story for us to focus on and often gives new understanding about it.

PREACHING / TEACHING: God anoints someone to speak or write about His word and often releases knowledge, revelation and understanding in the preaching of the word.

PROPHECY: He anoints another person to encourage and equip you for your future by giving new insight through a word they speak over you.

WORDS OF KNOWLEDGE: pieces of information are given from God to you or another person, that only God could know, to increase your faith for what He is saying or doing.

DREAMS: truths are conveyed to you while you are sleeping, often in the form of symbolic pictures or stories.

VISIONS: very similar to dreams, except you are awake. In your mind you see a series of images like a movie that is often in symbolic language that needs interpretation.

OPEN VISIONS: same as a vision except you see it with your eyes, not as a mental image.

TRANCES: like an open vision but with added interaction and the fading away of your current environment.

TONGUES AND INTERPRETATION: direct communication from the Holy Spirit via a heavenly language that requires a spiritual translation to be understood.

TONGUES: a version of speaking in tongues different than our personal prayer language in which someone speaks or writes in another earthly language that he or she does not know but those listening do.

IMPRESSIONS: perhaps the most common way God talks. A person gets a mental picture, word or phrase, scripture reference, song, or other thought that did not originate from them but from God.

INTERNAL VOICE: you "hear" God speaking to you something, but the voice is internal and can not be heard by others.

AUDIBLE VOICE: He speaks out loud so that one or more persons can hear Him with their ears.

INSPIRATION: God releases grace and revelation through music, art or nature in which no actual words were exchanged but the message is heard.

MANIFESTATIONS: these are not words but communication via physical, emotional or spiritual feelings or sensations.

ANGELS: God sends a message by a heavenly messenger in a dream, vision or actual visitation.

TESTIMONIES: when God does something for someone else and we hear about it, the testimony of what God did is prophesying that He wants to do the same for us.

MIRACLES: like testimonies but done through our own hands. When God does something through us He is not just doing something but also communicating to us so that we think differently after the miracle than before.

This list is not comprehensive or limiting, but simple descriptions of some of the ways God speaks. Hopefully, as you read this list your faith and revelation will increase and you will begin to set your heart and mind to hear and understand more than ever before. The value of the truth God is communicating is not defined by how dramatically He speaks. Sometimes the open vision, audible voice or angelic visitation is given because the message is important, but sometimes it is just because that is the only way it would be heard. Do not discount a dream or impression because it is not as dramatic. Value and honor every word and you will find yourself not only hearing more but understanding more as well.

[Jhn 10:27 NKJV] 27 "My sheep hear My voice, and I know them, and they follow Me.

THE RENEWED MIND

[Rom 12:2 NKJV] 2 And do not be conformed to this world, but be transformed by the renewing of your mind, that you may prove what [is] that good and acceptable and perfect will of God.

You know your mind is renewed when you think like God, when what others think is impossible seems perfectly logical to you, and when you can show others what God's will is, not just talk about it. Remember the parable of the sower and the seed in Matthew 13. Jesus said that it was the foundational parable that would be the key to understanding everything else. How we receive what God says and the effects that word has on our hearts and mind is an essential aspect of the Christian life.

[Mat 13:23 NKJV] 23 "But he who received seed on the good ground is he who hears the word and understands [it], who indeed bears fruit and produces: some a hundredfold, some sixty, some thirty."

That is the picture of the renewed mind. The word is received, understood, and bearing fruit in our lives.

The renewing of our mind is the means by which we are transformed. Our inner man grows and changes until it begins to resemble the kingdom of heaven. He talks, we listen and respond, and we are transformed on the inside. When our minds are renewed all the obstacles to faith are removed and the things of heaven flow freely to us and through us.

[Eph 4:21-23 NKJV] 21 if indeed you have heard Him and have been taught by Him, as the truth is in Jesus: 22 that you put off, concerning your former conduct, the old man which grows corrupt according to the deceitful lusts, 23 and be renewed in the spirit of your mind,

Everything we want as believers in Jesus; answered prayer, maturity, fruitfulness, miracles, strong relationships, and so on, is not magically given to us fully formed and ready to use. It is made possible through this renewing of the mind process that this chapter is all about. It is the only way that we can demonstrate God's will in our own lives and the lives of others. Many people think that when bad things happen it must be the will of God because He is all powerful and allowed it to happen. But they have ignored the process by which His will was to be made known. His will is good and the only way it is manifested in our lives is when our minds are renewed and there is a channel through which He can demonstrate His goodness. Begin today to treasure His word within you and be transformed so that you can be that channel.

FAITH

CHAPTER 3

NOTHING SHALL BE IMPOSSIBLE

[Mat 17:19-20 NKJV] 19 Then the disciples came to Jesus privately and said, "Why could we not cast it out?" 20 So Jesus said to them, "Because of your unbelief; for assuredly, I say to you, if you have faith as a mustard seed, you will say to this mountain, 'Move from here to there,' and it will move; and nothing will be impossible for you.

THE FAITH OF GOD

[Mar 11:22 YLT] 22 And Jesus answering saith to them, `Have faith of God;

Now that we have a better understanding of what faith is and how we increase it in our personal life, let us explore how faith works in our circumstances and ministries. Faith is not a feeling. It is not a human emotion that comes and goes, nor is it generated from inside of us. Faith, like everything else that is good, begins with God. Faith is a response to the revelation of who God is, to the knowledge of what God is saying, and to the anointing on our life or the life of another. Essentially, faith starts with God and grows as we respond to Him.

Most people when tasked with getting more faith to accomplish something impossible by human effort turn to trying harder or striving. But faith does not grow through more effort because it is not of human origin. Believing God is much more an act of yielding to God than it is demanding or working. Faith is a position of confident rest in His character, word, and power. It originates with God, therefore it is His faith, not ours. He is

44

the faithful One just like He is love, peace, joy, and hope. So we rest in His ability as we learn how to get things done in our lives and the lives of others.

YOU WILL HAVE WHATEVER YOU SAY

[Mar 11:23-24 NKJV] 23 "For assuredly, I say to you, whoever says to this mountain, 'Be removed and be cast into the sea,' and does not doubt in his heart, but believes that those things he says will be done, he will have whatever he says. 24 "Therefore I say to you, whatever things you ask when you pray, believe that you receive [them], and you will have [them].

[Rom 10:9-10 NKJV] 9 that if you confess with your mouth the Lord Jesus and believe in your heart that God has raised Him from the dead, you will be saved. 10 For with the heart one believes unto righteousness, and with the mouth confession is made unto salvation.

[Luk 11:9 NKJV] 9 "So I say to you, ask, and it will be given to you; seek, and you will find; knock, and it will be opened to you.

[Luk 18:6-8 NKJV] 6 Then the Lord said, "Hear what the unjust judge said. 7 "And shall God not avenge His own elect who cry out day and night to Him, though He bears long with them? 8 "I tell you that He will avenge them speedily. Nevertheless, when the Son of Man comes, will He really find faith on the earth?"

The nature of faith is trust and confidence that grows in your heart and is expressed through your mouth. To imply that you can believe something in your heart that does not come out of your mouth is misleading. Faith is authoritative in nature and that means you have delegated authority on earth to demonstrate God's will through your mouth. You have a place of intimate relationship to the King from which you ask, confess, and decree the things of heaven into your reality. Again, faith is confident asking and declaring with the backing of heaven that move things on earth. Talking is required.

Some things in the kingdom you can only get by asking for them. No amount of good performance, begging, or demanding will produce the desired result. Why? Because God is a good Father who can not be manipulated, and who does not respond to need but to faith. We are not orphans begging to be noticed. Nor are we spoiled brats throwing a tantrum to get our way. It will not work.

God requires that we come to Him as sons and daughters. Kicking and screaming does not move Him, confidence in what Jesus did and who we are because of it does. He requires that we approach Him as a good Father, knowing that He is both all powerful and infinitely loving and always does what is best. We do not come to Him with accusation or unbelief. God requires that we take the time to search out through His word and revelation from the Spirit what His will is. We are not lazy prayers, who approach the Almighty like orphans with accusations in our hearts and begging on our lips. Nothing good will come of that.

So when we pray, how do we ask? First, we must approach God as a good Father. Nothing can replace time and relationship with Him that results in confidence in who He is. Next, we come to Him with gratefulness and worship. He deserves it and just like any good Father He is attracted to a thankful heart. It is not enough to know who He is however, we must know who we are. Believing in God has never been enough, we must believe in Jesus, and that means we believe in what He did for us. He brought us close to the Father as sons and we must act like sons to please Him. A solid place to ask from would not be complete without one more piece, and that is forgiveness. He paid our debt that was separating us from Him, and He expects us to do the same for others. We can not approach with confidence when we have not forgiven those who have wronged us.

Now that the foundational position from which we ask is in place, we move on to the act of praying. When we are requesting something from heaven, it is paramount that we know that what we are asking for is based on His promises. Our words have confidence because they are based on His words. Take the time before you ask to find a solid promise in the scripture and from the Spirit to base your request on. Do not rush into asking, just saying words in the air with no knowledge of who you are talking to or if what you are asking for is legal. Jesus died to give you both an inheritance and authority, and knowing His will in any situation is what gives you confidence when you are asking. The prayers that get answered are the ones He wanted to do before you asked.

Next, say the words out loud. Talk to a real God with real words based on real promises out loud and believe that you received what you asked for. Your voice matters. There is authority in what you say, so make it count.

Be persistent. Not begging persistent or religious persistent, but believing persistent. He is good, you are close to Him, He made the promise, and you asked for it. Then time passes and you do not see anything happen. Do not go back in doubt and question if He is good or your position or His promise. Simply keep asking with persistence believing that you get what you ask for. There are often details that we do not understand and mystery to live with. Do not get caught up in trying to figure all that out. Just ask, keep asking, believe and receive what you asked for.

Asking in this way is how we receive many things in the kingdom, but not all. In Luke 18 persistent asking is called faith by Jesus, but in Luke 8 He had a different response.

[Luk 8:24-25 NKJV] 24 And they came to Him and awoke Him, saying, "Master, Master, we are perishing!" Then He arose and rebuked the wind and the raging of the water. And they ceased, and there was a calm. 25 But He said to them, "Where is your faith?" And they were afraid, and marveled, saying to one another, "Who can this be? For He commands even the winds and water, and they obey Him!"

The disciples came to Him asking for help and He answered their prayer, but then rebuked them for their lack of faith. He expected them, after what they had experienced with Him, to speak to the storm themselves. In this case, asking was not faith, declaration was.

When we ask for something and we get it, He expects us to act like we have it. If He anoints us and commands us to do something He expects us to do it, not to keep asking. For example, Jesus never asked God to heal someone. He spoke with authority directly to the disease or demon and made it leave. Why? Because God had already anointed Him to heal and with that comes the authority to speak on His behalf. When we know His will and have His anointing, it is no longer faith to request something He already gave us.

Faith filled declarations are the way we execute His will on the earth. He told us to heal the sick and cast out demons, so we no longer talk to Him about that but to the thing standing in the way of His will. He said He would supply our needs, so we stop begging Him and start joining Him in creating what we need. So what do we ask for, and what do we make declarations about? Two things that we have biblical permission to ask for are more Holy Spirit (anointing) and more revelation. We need encounters with God to transfer things from heaven to us, and He said that He gives the Holy Spirit to those who ask Him. He wants a dialogue about that because He wants the relationship where we are continually being filled with Him. But everything else: provision, healing, forgiveness, and so on are all covered in your inheritance. You do not need them, you need revelation that you already have them so that you can use your words to execute His will. So when we pray it sounds like Paul's prayer for the Ephesians:

[Eph 1:15-19 NKJV] 15 Therefore I also, after I heard of your faith in the Lord Jesus and your love for all the saints, 16 do not cease to give thanks for you, making mention of you in my prayers: 17 that the God of our Lord Jesus Christ, the Father of glory, may give to you the spirit of wisdom and revelation in the knowledge of Him, 18 the eyes of your understanding being enlightened; that you may know what is the hope of His calling, what are the riches of the glory of His inheritance in the saints, 19 and what [is] the exceeding greatness of His power toward us who believe, according to the working of His mighty power

THE GIFT OF FAITH

[1Co 12:8-10 NKJV] 8 for to one is given the word of wisdom through the Spirit, to another the word of knowledge through the same Spirit, 9 to another faith by the same Spirit, to another gifts of healings by the same Spirit, 10 to another the working of miracles, to another prophecy, to another discerning of spirits, to another [different] kinds of tongues, to another the interpretation of tongues.

God is really good at His job, way better than we think. Sometimes when we pray He answers us with an opportunity He does not want us to miss. To help us not to miss these opportunities He gives us everything we need to get the job done. The gift of faith is when He loans us His own faith for a while to get something done. Grace comes in the form of a spiritual gift that helps us get where we need to be. He tells us specific information as a word of knowledge and then gives us the gift of faith to believe for it, and all we have to do is be aware of what is going on and act.

Now this does not happen all the time. There is still value in seeking with diligence the things of the kingdom. But sometimes He gives you specific knowledge about circumstances or about people to bring about good, and knowing you or they need faith to accomplish it, He just gives it to you. Say thank you and run with it. Not everything is about your faith, or your diligence, or your experience; sometimes He just has compassion and lets you participate in what He is doing.

AGREEMENT

[Mat 18:18-19 NKJV] 18 "Assuredly, I say to you, whatever you bind on earth will be bound in heaven, and whatever you loose on earth will be loosed in heaven. 19 "Again I say to you that if two of you agree on earth concerning anything that they ask, it will be done for them by My Father in heaven.

[Jhn 20:23 NKJV] 23 "If you forgive the sins of any, they are forgiven them; if you retain the [sins] of any, they are retained."

There are two types of agreement that are important to understand as they both enhance our faith and get things done in the kingdom. First, there is our agreement with heaven. When we as a group or as individuals know our position seated with Him in heavenly places and our delegated authority on the earth, that agreement creates an environment that is extremely powerful. That understanding of our place in the authority structure of the kingdom releases power on the earth like little else. It is no longer just God forgiving, healing and restoring, but us too. We have authority to forgive sins, heal sickness, cast out demons, and release blessing. This is faith: knowing who we are and the power available and agreeing with God to do what He would do if He were here.

Secondly, there is an agreement between two or more people that, according to Jesus, guarantees an answer from heaven. If all else fails, you have done all you know to do and nothing is working, this is where you go. If you cannot feel the anointing, and nothing is falling into place, then find out what you, the bible, and the other person can agree on. Whether you have to build up their faith or lower yours, find a place where you can meet. Take a clear promise from the scripture and both of you find your lowest common denominator around it and start there. Guaranteed win. Then your faith will grow and you can agree for more until you have whatever you need.

ACTIVE FAITH

[Jhn 9:7 NKJV] 7 And He said to him, "Go, wash in the pool of Siloam" (which is translated, Sent). So he went and washed, and came back seeing.

Take a look through the gospels at the miracles Jesus did when He was one on one with people. Very often He gave them something to do to activate their faith. Faith needs something to do. We discussed already how faith needs to say something, but sometimes faith needs to do something. When you are believing God for a miracle, He will likely prompt you to take some action that demonstrates and activates your faith. It is like your faith is growing in your heart but it does not produce the desired result until you move.

Similarly, when God is using you to do a miracle for someone else, He will often prompt you to give them something to do to activate their faith. They may need a healing and you pray for them but they do not receive it until they try to do what they could not before. Perhaps just standing up, or walking forward, or releasing forgiveness is what will activate their faith. Be sensitive to the Holy Spirit about this and encourage them to do the same. We often do not know if we believe something until we say it and do it.

Mark 11 says that when you pray you should believe that you receive when you pray. Not that you will receive it, but that you did receive it. That posture of the heart that believes you already got what you prayed for needs to be expressed. We do that by thanking God for giving it to us, and by acting like we have it. For example, say you asked Him for the anointing to heal the sick. Believe that He gave it to you, thank Him for it, and start praying for the sick. Do something that demonstrates what you believe.

DRAWING ON THE ANOINTING

[Heb 11:1 NKJV] 1 Now faith is the substance of things hoped for, the evidence of things not seen.

As we will learn in the upcoming chapters, the atmosphere that is hope is the same as that of the anointing. It is the environment where anything is possible. The anointing is what makes hope possible. When God wants to get something done or bless a group of people, He anoints someone to do it. That means he delegates to that person some of Jesus' authority and covers them with the Holy Spirit so that they have what they need to accomplish His will. We are not anointed for ourselves, but so that He can bless others through us.

When we recognize and honor the anointing on someone's life, it gives us access to heaven through them. Faith can draw the blessing of God through them into you. This is demonstrated all through the gospels. Jesus Christ, whose very name means the Anointed One, comes into a town. He starts by proclaiming who He is as the anointed of the Holy Spirit. Those who honor Him for who He is gain access to that anointing through faith. This is why He could say that they only needed a little bit of faith to see amazing miracles. Where there is plenty of anointing you only need a little faith, but where there is very little anointing you need more faith. If there is neither faith nor anointing, God's desire to bless His people does not happen.

Faith gives substance or demonstration to what we are anointed to do. God rests His Spirit on us for the sake of others. Faith recognizes that Spirit and does not discredit it because of the weak human who is carrying it. Faith realizes that with the anointing of the Spirit anything is possible, but does not settle for anything being possible. It draws on the anointing to get a specific thing done in a specific time - now. Remember the woman with the issue of blood. She recognized the anointing on Jesus, demonstrated her faith by what she said and did, and drew on the anointing with her faith to get her miracle.

Let us use our faith through our words, actions, agreement, honor, and the gifts He gives us to prove His will on the earth and see many people blessed because of it.

HOPE

CHAPTER 4

YOU SHALL RECEIVE POWER

[Luk 24:49 NKJV] 49 "Behold, I send the Promise of My Father upon you; but tarry in the city of Jerusalem until you are endued with power from on high."

[Act 1:8 NKJV] 8 "But you shall receive power when the Holy Spirit has come upon you; and you shall be witnesses to Me in Jerusalem, and in all Judea and Samaria, and to the end of the earth."

THINGS HOPED FOR

[Rom 15:13 NKJV] 13 Now may the God of hope fill you with all joy and peace in believing, that you may abound in hope by the power of the Holy Spirit.

Hope is the joyful anticipation of good. It is expecting good things to happen in the future. The atmosphere or environment called hope is a powerful momentum building environment that draws people into the kingdom. When there is hope it feels like anything is possible, and that is both a fun and powerful place to be. So what creates hope? The anointing of the Holy Spirit.

The next few chapters we are going to dive into the realm of hope, but not what it is so much as where it comes from. The power that comes upon us through the anointing of the Holy Spirit is what makes hope possible, for without the anointing we do not have a reason to expect good. When the Spirit of God comes upon a person they are now empowered to accomplish the task God has asked them to do. There are things God wants to do among us, the things hoped for mentioned in Hebrews 11:1, and to do them He anoints someone.

[Heb 11:1 NKJV] 1 Now faith is the substance of things hoped for, the evidence of things not seen.

The things that are hoped for are the things God has anointed us to do, and the anointing mixed with faith is what brings substance to the expectations of God. When we carry both the heart and the power of the Spirit, we carry the works of God, and faith draws those things from the realm of the Spirit into reality.

AMBASSADORS

[Jhn 15:15-16 NKJV] 15 "No longer do I call you servants, for a servant does not know what his master is doing; but I have called you friends, for all things that I heard from My Father I have made known to you. 16 "You did not choose Me, but I chose you and appointed you that you should go and bear fruit, and [that] your fruit should remain, that whatever you ask the Father in My name He may give you.

[Jhn 15:26-27 NKJV] 26 "But when the Helper comes, whom I shall send to you from the Father, the Spirit of truth who proceeds from the Father, He will testify of Me. 27 "And you also will bear witness, because you have been with Me from the beginning.

To be anointed by God for ministry is essentially God trusting you with an assignment. When He puts His Spirit on you, He is actually delegating part of His authority to you to accomplish part of the task of bringing the kingdom to the earth. When we enter the kingdom, it is always by humbly surrendering to the lordship of Jesus and believing in who He is and what He has done for us. Although we are immediately adopted as sons and have access to the heart of God, trust is something that is built over time. We are His servants, believing and doing what He says without much understanding of why or how. But as we grow and mature, He begins to call us friends, trusting us with more of His heart.

People are what God is all about. He loves people and longs to bring wholeness to them in every area of life. Jesus was anointed to begin the task of bringing wholeness to everyone on earth that would accept Him, and He has been delegating some of that job to others ever since. The anointing for ministry comes when God trusts us with some of those people. He pours out His Spirit on us and empowers us to do part of His job on the earth. Without the anointing there is no fruit, no power, no ministry.

Jesus is the King, and He sends us as His friends and ambassadors to represent Him to others. He tasks us with the mission of being His representative in a church, city, region, or nation. As we represent Him to others well, He expands our sphere of influence. Our influence only extends to those whom we have a genuine love for and those we are willing to take responsibility for. To allow us to demonstrate accurately His heart and will for the people we influence, He places the anointing of the Spirit on us. His Spirit gives us the love, revelation, boldness, and power we need to do what He would do if He were there.

THE ANOINTED ONE

[Luk 3:21-22 NKJV] 21 When all the people were baptized, it came to pass that Jesus also was baptized; and while He prayed, the heaven was opened. 22 And the Holy Spirit descended in bodily form like a dove upon Him, and a voice came from heaven which said, "You are My beloved Son; in You I am well pleased."

[Luk 4:1 NKJV] 1 Then Jesus, being filled with the Holy Spirit, returned from the Jordan and was led by the Spirit into the wilderness

[Luk 4:14 NKJV] 14 Then Jesus returned in the power of the Spirit to Galilee, and news of Him went out through all the surrounding region.

[Luk 4:17-21 NKJV] 17 And He was handed the book of the prophet Isaiah. And when He had opened the book, He found the place where it was written: 18 "The Spirit of the LORD [is] upon Me, Because He has anointed Me To preach the gospel to [the] poor; He has sent Me to heal the brokenhearted, To proclaim liberty to [the] captives And recovery of sight to [the] blind, To set at liberty those who are oppressed; 19 To proclaim the acceptable year of the LORD." 20 Then He closed the book, and gave [it] back to the attendant and sat down. And the eyes of all who were in the synagogue were fixed on Him. 21 And He began to say to them, "Today this Scripture is fulfilled in your hearing."

[Luk 3:16 NKJV] 16 John answered, saying to all, "I indeed baptize you with water; but One mightier than I is coming, whose sandal strap I am not worthy to loose. He will baptize you with the Holy Spirit and fire.

The Christ. Jesus Christ has many titles and many roles as the Messiah. He is fully God at the same time He is fully man. The sacrifice for sin, High Priest, and King are some of His roles in our redemption. He is prophet, teacher, and head of the church. But as a man His primary title is "The Christ." It means the Anointed One. Jesus did all of His earthly ministry voluntarily as a man who was anointed by the Spirit. He is both our example and our means to Godly character and powerful ministry.

We are not just forgiven by God and on our way to heaven. We are a part of a kingdom that is advancing with Jesus as our model for life and ministry. Healing of all diseases, wholeness for every broken heart, forgiveness for every sin, freedom from every demon, and restoration for every relationship is not just our inheritance, it is our mandate and responsibility. Jesus is the anointed one and He paved the way for us to be anointed. He is the sent one and now we are the same. He was empowered by the Spirit not just to do good things, but to open the heavens for us to be empowered by the same Spirit. He is our model.

Just as Jesus yielded to the love of the Father and the leading of the Spirit, we must do the same. He became completely dependent on His relationship with the Father through the Spirit. He surrendered to the fasting in the wilderness and came out in the power of the Spirit. Confidently He proclaimed the anointing on His life even while being extremely humble as a man. It was not self promotion, but faith in what the Father had deposited on His life. We must follow His example of surrender and faith and put our trust completely in the work of the Spirit. As we grow in our trust of Him, He will trust us with more power to follow the example that He set for us.

"Come to Me and drink," Jesus said in John 7, and "rivers of living water will flow from you." Jesus is the Anointed One and the one who anoints us. He was baptized in the Spirit and He is the one who baptizes us in both the Holy Spirit and fire. We must come to Him and learn from Him and ask Him to baptize us in the Spirit. When we are saved, He comes into our hearts, cleanses us, and provides the grace for us to live in the kingdom. But there is more. He wants to cover us with the Spirit for the sake of others. It was never about just getting enough to get by, it was drinking from Jesus so that we become a source of life for those around us.

EVIDENCE OF THE ANOINTING

[Act 4:29-30 NKJV] 29 "Now, Lord, look on their threats, and grant to Your servants that with all boldness they may speak Your word, 30 "by stretching out Your hand to heal, and that signs and wonders may be done through the name of Your holy Servant Jesus."

"Give us more" was the disciples response in Acts four after tasting of the outpouring of the Spirit in chapter two and the effects it had on them. They got more and continued to proclaim the good news of Jesus and demonstrate it with power. We need more as well. We should never be satisfied with what we have but instead continue to ask and yield for more of the anointing.

So what are we looking for? What does it mean to be anointed? At the core of it, being anointed is being empowered to bless the lives of others. It is God clothing you with His Spirit so that together you can change people's lives. It sounds kind of mysterious, but there are some common evidences that make it easier to understand. This list is not to contain the anointing, but to describe some of the basic evidence that it is at work in someone's life.

Boldness is the first and most common evidence across the board. Everyone empowered by the Spirit gets a dramatic increase in

69

boldness. This is not a personality trait, as many people who have tasted of this retained an introverted personality. Rather, it is an increased confidence to speak and act for the Lord because of the anointing.

Love is next. Not sentiment or pity, but genuine love from God. Those who are baptized by the Spirit begin to feel as He feels about people, and God loves people. Forgiveness comes easier, enjoyment is more natural, and compassion flows through those who are anointed.

Revelation. One of the clearest signs of the anointing is the increase in one's ability to hear, understand and speak the voice of God. People begin to prophesy, dream, hear His voice, see visions and so on in a greater way after the anointing comes.

Miracles also dramatically increase because of the baptism of the Spirit. Any believer through faith in the word or agreement can access the miraculous, but the anointing makes it feel easier and more frequent. Healing, creative miracles, provision, and deliverance is what He does, and when He comes on us, that is what we do.

Speaking in tongues. One of the first signs of the baptism for many is the establishment of a special communication between God and us called tongues. It could be a prayer language by which our spirit communicates with His, a prophetic language that declares things to others, another human language that we do not naturally speak, or all of the above. It is an important part of our life and ministry and should not be despised or ignored, but it is not by itself the evidence of the anointing. There should be other evidence like boldness, love and power, not just tongues.

Let us follow the example of Jesus and pursue the anointing of the Holy Spirit for the sake of the world around us.

HOPE

CHAPTER 5

THERE'S MORE!

[1Co 14:1 YLT] 1 Pursue the love, and seek earnestly the spiritual things, and rather that ye may prophesy

[Eph 5:18-19 NKJV] 18 And do not be drunk with wine, in which is dissipation; but be filled with the Spirit, 19 speaking to one another in psalms and hymns and spiritual songs, singing and making melody in your heart to the Lord

SEEK EARNESTLY THE SPIRITUAL

Nothing is more valuable than the anointing of the Holy Spirit. It is the grace that changes us on the inside, and it is the power that flows through us to the world around. The anointing is the means by which heaven is transferred to the earth. That being true, the question is how do you become anointed, and once you are, how do you get more?

First, it is important to know that there is more. Wherever you are in the kingdom, there is always more. God would not tell us to earnestly seek something that He does not intend to give those who seek. There is always more. So how do we get it? There are no magic words, special rituals, rules to keep, or formulas because the "it" we are after is not an "it" but a Him. The anointing is not a substance but a person who is God and cannot be manipulated. He will not be owned or controlled, only yielded to.

Only through relationship, surrender and obedience do we find what we are looking for. There are no shortcuts. Some things you can only find seeking Him alone in the secret place, while others can only be found in corporate worship. Sometimes hunger and persistence are needed, while other times rest and enjoyment are the keys. Is it the laying on of hands, prophecy, impartation, manifestations or personal encounters? All of the above. Do we honor those who are anointed and follow their lead or do we launch out on our own and risk everything? Both. There are many ways in which the Holy Spirit gains access to us and we gain access to Him, but all of them require humility and a hearing ear.

We are going to talk about some of the essential ways the anointing is increased in our lives, but it is critical to note that He will not be boxed in. The important things are yieldedness, hunger, patience, enjoyment, surrender, persistence, and honor. By the time you are the anointed of the Lord, you will be His yielded friend leaning on Him for everything. There are no exceptions.

ENCOUNTERS

[Act 2:1-4 NKJV] 1 When the Day of Pentecost had fully come, they were all with one accord in one place. 2 And suddenly there came a sound from heaven, as of a rushing mighty wind, and it filled the whole house where they were sitting. 3 Then there appeared to them divided tongues, as of fire, and [one] sat upon each of them. 4 And they were all filled with the Holy Spirit and began to speak with other tongues, as the Spirit gave them utterance.

[Act 4:31 NKJV] 31 And when they had prayed, the place where they were assembled together was shaken; and they were all filled with the Holy Spirit, and they spoke the word of God with boldness.

[Act 13:52 NKJV] 52 And the disciples were filled with joy and with the Holy Spirit.

Encounter is a word that has many meanings, but essentially it is when the Spirit of God manifests Himself to you in a way that changes you. It may be a love encounter where He brings wholeness to some broken part of you, or a power encounter where you are left lying on the floor in a heap with electricity flowing through your body. Sometimes it is through revelation and inspired thoughts, and sometimes it is through weeping or laughing.

God changes us not through our own will power but through close contact between ourselves and Him. He is relational in nature and He loves to talk to us, be with us, and touch us. If there are any lines that we are not willing to cross or any place where we will not let Him in, then we are limiting how much we are willing to carry of Him. For example, if we are comfortable with Him touching our heart so that tears begin to flow, but not with Him causing us to laugh, then we have determined our ceiling. If we care more about our reputation than Him so that we are embarrassed by His touch, then we set the parameters of how much we want.

Everyone throughout history who has carried the anointing has come to a place where they valued it more than anything. Many say "why do I have to go over there, God knows where I am," and their limit is set by their own stubborn pride. Others refuse to make time to sit in the secret place therefore restricting themselves by their impatience. But the hungry will go wherever they need to go, sit as long as it takes, and yield whatever is required. How far are you willing to go?

Being filled with the Spirit is not a one time experience but a lifestyle of encounter. It is the yielded life in which nothing is off limits to our Savior that makes all the difference. We cannot cause an encounter with God, but rather we position ourselves so that we are ready when He comes. Be willing to go to corporate worship meetings when many are staying home. There are some things you cannot get on your own. Let the Word of God wash and cleanse you, never changing it to suit you, but changing yourself to suit it. Set aside hours and days to be with Him with no agenda in a time where busyness is the norm.

Go wherever you need to go to experience His presence. Yield any habit or thought pattern that He does not like. Listen to those who have walked in the anointing and honor them. Go hungry if you have to. Be quick to obey His promptings, and be willing to live with mystery. What if your church tradition says that the gifts of the Spirit are for another day and speaking in tongues is not necessary? Then you will have to decide if your traditions will be your ceiling, or if you will seek the truth. Ask for more, and if you do not hear an answer then ask again. Do whatever it takes.

Value the anointing of the Holy Spirit more than anything in life. Seek, yield, hunger, enjoy, believe, endure and trust. Do not put a limit on your life for any reason. For all those who seek will find.

IMPARTATION

[Act 8:17 NKJV] 17 Then they laid hands on them, and they received the Holy Spirit.

[Act 19:6 NKJV] 6 And when Paul had laid hands on them, the Holy Spirit came upon them, and they spoke with tongues and prophesied.

[Rom 1:11 NKJV] 11 For I long to see you, that I may impart to you some spiritual gift, so that you may be established

[2Ti 1:6 NKJV] 6 Therefore I remind you to stir up the gift of God which is in you through the laying on of my hands.

[Jhn 20:22 NKJV] 22 And when He had said this, He breathed on [them], and said to them, "Receive the Holy Spirit.

There are some things in the kingdom that you cannot get directly from God, but must be transferred through the laying on of hands. God has designed a system of government that promotes interdependence, love and humility. On purpose, He reserves some of what you need in the lives of the fathers and leaders He has set over you. If you are going to walk in all He has for your life, then you must be willing to seek those people out and have them release from heaven what God has in store for you.

Identify those who carry the anointing and the authority of the kingdom. They will be the ones giving their life away in love, taking responsibility to bring wholeness to others, and moving in the power of God. Do not go after those who can talk well but cannot back it up with power, nor go after those whose lives are controlled by selfishness. Find the fathers and mothers of the faith no matter their age or fame, and ask them to pray for you. If you do not know anyone like that, then widen your scope. Ask the Lord to help you find someone and be willing to travel.

You do not have to have a relationship with them in order for God to use them to touch you. They are similar to a mailman in this case, delivering to you what the Father desires to give. It is your faith, hunger, humility, and honor that draws on the anointing on their life and gets you more. The gifts that you receive through their prayer of impartation is not limited to what they carry themselves.

Rather, God is giving you the gifts and callings He wants you to have and He is using them as the delivery system.

It is important to note that you will not get everything this way. You have to build your own history with God, love others, and obey. Only you can develop intimacy between yourself and the Lord. It is also important to remember that many things we get from the Lord do not come fully formed, but in seed form. When He gives us the promise of an oak tree it usually comes in the form of an acorn that we grow with Him through faith and patience.

HONORING THE ANOINTED

[Act 10:44 NKJV] 44 While Peter was still speaking these words, the Holy Spirit fell upon all those who heard the word.

[Jhn 3:34 NKJV] 34 "For He whom God has sent speaks the words of God, for God does not give the Spirit by measure.

[Jhn 6:63 NKJV] 63 "It is the Spirit who gives life; the flesh profits nothing. The words that I speak to you are spirit, and [they] are life.

[1Co 2:4 NKJV] 4 And my speech and my preaching [were] not with persuasive words of human wisdom, but in demonstration of the Spirit and of power

[Mat 10:41 NKJV] 41 "He who receives a prophet in the name of a prophet shall receive a prophet's reward. And he who receives a righteous man in the name of a righteous man shall receive a righteous man's reward.

One of the most amazing things about the anointing is how it can be transferred. People were healed by touching Jesus' clothes, demons left people when a cloth from Paul touched them, and just by saying a command people were touched miles away. Sometimes there was not even any contact or words, just honor that produced faith that pulled the anointing into a situation.

When someone carries the anointing of God for something, the kingdom is available for us to access through them. But the access is not automatic. There are specific ways that the transfer of the anointing is made possible and all of them require honor. Honor in this sense is not acting noble or doing the right thing, but giving proper respect to what God has deposited in another person.

When I am seeking the Lord and asking for something, many times He answers by depositing what I need in another person. For example, if I am seeking for an increase in the spiritual gift of words of knowledge, God's response will be to prompt me to listen to someone who flows in that gift. If I am willing and able to recognize what that person carries spiritually and honor them for it, them some of what they have can be transferred to me. The Spirit is actually carried in their words, and through honor I can access Him and get what I need. To expect that God will answer all of our prayers with fully formed mature answers delivered directly to us is not realistic. God often answers us in a way that requires us to grow in faith, love, and interdependence in order to receive the answer so that we are mature enough to use what we get. This works with people we know, as well as with people we do not. Even those who have already died can carry the anointing in their written or spoken words. Honor unlocks the anointing and releases it to us.

The anointing is not just for platform ministry. God anoints people for creativity, making money, building relationships, leadership, and many other things. If you ask for something, many times your answer will come in the form of a friend or acquaintance. Say you need financial help. You pray, give, and work, everything you know to do, but you still have needs that are not met. Many times

God will bring into your life someone who is financially successful. If your response to them is jealousy or self-pity, then you do not get what you need, but if you recognize what they carry and honor them for it, then your answers are unlocked. The same is true for healing and breakthrough in many areas of life.

God loves family, love, humility and respect. He loves leaders who serve and servants who honor. He has designed His kingdom to require and empower those things in us. Many times God has been blamed for not answering a prayer when it was our own narrow focus that kept us from the answer. The way of the kingdom is to love the Lord with all of our heart, soul, mind, and strength and to love our neighbor as ourselves. Sometimes that means worshiping Him in secret, fasting and prayer, and studying the scriptures. Other times it will mean traveling to another city to seek what He is doing there or listening to an anointed preacher. It may be recognizing the Spirit on a friend or even a stranger, or allowing Him to use us to touch the poor. Whether we are the one carrying the anointing or the one seeking, it is the yielded life that gets more of God.

HOPE

CHAPTER 6

HOSTING HIS PRESENCE

[Isa 11:2 NKJV] 2 The Spirit of the LORD shall rest upon Him, The Spirit of wisdom and understanding, The Spirit of counsel and might, The Spirit of knowledge and of the fear of the LORD.

HOSTING THE DOVE

[Rom 8:5-6 NKJV] 5 For those who live according to the flesh set their minds on the things of the flesh, but those [who live] according to the Spirit, the things of the Spirit. 6 For to be carnally minded [is] death, but to be spiritually minded [is] life and peace.

[Jhn 1:32 NKJV] 32 And John bore witness, saying, "I saw the Spirit descending from heaven like a dove, and He remained upon Him.

At the center of this book is perhaps the most important subject of them all, hosting the presence of the Holy Spirit. It was what Jesus was exceptionally good at, and it is what every person who shaped the course of history for God learned to do. Nothing else matters if we do not get this. Much of what I have learned on this matter came from Bill Johnson. He has not only taught on this in depth but also demonstrated it in a way that few others have, and for that I honor him.

When Jesus was baptized in water the Father publicly blessed Him and then the Holy Spirit descended on Him in the form of a dove and remained. This chapter is about that concept of the Spirit of God coming on someone and remaining. Forget the symbolism for a moment of why the Spirit was in the form of a dove, and think about the reality. If there were a real dove on your shoulder and you wanted it to stay, how would you act? The dove would have to be the first priority on your mind, every minute of every day. You are not capturing the dove, He is there voluntarily, so you can not make Him stay. Every decision you made would have to be with Him in mind in order to create the environment that motivated Him to remain.

Awareness of the anointing is the first key to walking in it. As we saw in Romans 8 above it is the act of setting our mind on the things of the Spirit that leads to an atmosphere of life and peace, and that is the atmosphere in which the anointing flourishes. We honor the Holy Spirit as a person who is God by staying aware of who He is, what He is capable of, and recognizing that He has chosen to rest upon us. Never take it lightly that He has chosen us, never underestimate Him, and always set our mind on Him throughout the day. As simple as it sounds, this is the first and foremost step in hosting His presence.

By simply taking the time to think about Him we enter into fellowship with His heart. We honor Him by acknowledging His presence with gratefulness and awareness. If I am with someone, how can I make them feel honored? They will feel honored when I listen to what they say with care, when I am genuinely glad that they are with me, when I pay close attention to their desires, and when I recognize the importance of the gifts and talents they have. It is the same with the Holy Spirit. If we ignore Him, we dishonor Him and He has no reason to stay, but if we properly host Him with the honor He deserves, He remains.

HOSTING THE FIRE

[1Th 5:19 NKJV] 19 Do not quench the Spirit.

[Lev 6:13 NKJV] 13 'A fire shall always be burning on the altar; it shall never go out.

[Rom 12:1 NKJV] 1 I beseech you therefore, brethren, by the mercies of God, that you present your bodies a living sacrifice, holy, acceptable to God, [which is] your reasonable service.

To quench means to put the fire out. It can imply purposeful action like pouring water on it, but it also can mean neglectful inaction like starving it out by not supplying enough fuel. All you have to do to put out a fire is not feed it. The Spirit of God is a fire that rests on people who will be a living sacrifice, because fire always falls on sacrifice.

When Jesus was filled with the Holy Spirit, the first thing He did was follow the leading of the Spirit into the wilderness. He yielded so beautifully to the will of the Father and became a sacrifice that the fire could fall on. Afterwards He came out of the wilderness in the power of the Spirit, and breakthrough for that region and the world began. But Jesus did not ever stop yielding. He kept an attitude of humility and surrender that attracted the fire of God His whole life.

This is the life that not only attracts the Holy Spirit but continues to attract Him, the yielded life. Not just a one time surrender, but an ongoing sacrifice that He can burn. We keep putting wood on the altar of our lives by daily saying yes to Him no matter what He asks of us. It is the quick and joyful obedience of everything He prompts us to do, no matter the cost, that keeps the fire burning. Yield, it is the only way. He will not share control with you, so if you take control you are asking Him to leave. Sacrifice is the means to keeping the fire burning.

HOSTING THE RIVER

[Jhn 7:37-39 NKJV] 37 On the last day, that great [day] of the feast, Jesus stood and cried out, saying, "If anyone thirsts, let him come to Me and drink. 38 "He who believes in Me, as the Scripture has said, out of his heart will flow rivers of living water." 39 But this He spoke concerning the Spirit, whom those believing in Him would receive; for the Holy Spirit was not yet [given], because Jesus was not yet glorified.

[Eph 4:29-32 NKJV] 29 Let no corrupt word proceed out of your mouth, but what is good for necessary edification, that it may impart grace to the hearers. 30 And do not grieve the Holy Spirit of God, by whom you were sealed for the day of redemption. 31 Let all bitterness, wrath, anger, clamor, and evil speaking be put away from you, with all malice. 32 And be kind to one another, tenderhearted, forgiving one another, even as God in Christ forgave you.

[Isa 58:11 NKJV] 11 The LORD will guide you continually, And satisfy your soul in drought, And strengthen your bones; You shall be like a watered garden, And like a spring of water, whose waters do not fail.

The Spirit is a life giving river that flows from heaven to earth, and He wants to flow through you. By simply believing in Jesus and drinking from Him we not only get access to the Spirit, but others can access Him through us. Grace, power, life, forgiveness, mercy, peace, miracles, and provision all flowing right through us to those around us. We are the channel that He flows in and through.

Your life is like a pipe that the river of God runs through. As long as you stay clean and free from obstructions, He runs through you freely. But if you allow bitterness and anger to grow inside you, the flow of the river is diminished and can even be stopped. This is the picture of grieving the Spirit of God. He dwells in us for our benefit, but He flows through us for the benefit of others. Anger and bitterness restrict the flow to those around us, therefore restricting the anointing on our life.

God loves people. When we fail to love people because of bitterness or unforgiveness it is like a cancer that begins to grow on the inside. The diameter of our pipe shrinks as the bitterness grows, and the anointing begins to dry up. Not only does the river dry up, but the very heart of God is hurt. To grieve Him is to take His heart of love for people and restrict it through our anger towards those people. To host the presence of God is to be a vessel that is clean and free of bitterness. It is to allow the river to flow through us unrestricted.

BEING A GATE OF HEAVEN

[Gen 28:12, 17 NKJV] 12 Then he dreamed, and behold, a ladder [was] set up on the earth, and its top reached to heaven; and there the angels of God were ascending and descending on it. ... 17 And he was afraid and said, "How awesome [is] this place! This [is] none other than the house of God, and this [is] the gate of heaven!"

[Jhn 1:51 NKJV] 51 And He said to him, "Most assuredly, I say to you, hereafter you shall see heaven open, and the angels of God ascending and descending upon the Son of Man."

[Luk 3:21 NKJV] 21 When all the people were baptized, it came to pass that Jesus also was baptized; and while He prayed, the heaven was opened.

[Jhn 20:21 NKJV] 21 So Jesus said to them again, "Peace to you! As the Father has sent Me, I also send you."

[Eph 1:11-14 NKJV] 11 In Him also we have obtained an inheritance, being predestined according to the purpose of Him who works all things according to the counsel of His will, 12 that we who first trusted in Christ should be to the praise of His glory. 13 In Him you also [trusted], after you heard the word of truth, the gospel of your salvation; in whom also, having believed, you were sealed with the Holy Spirit of promise, 14 who is the guarantee of our inheritance until the redemption of the purchased possession, to the praise of His glory.

Heaven comes to earth through people. When the heavens were opened and the Spirit descended on Jesus, it was not a one time thing. Because of what He did the heavens remain open for us. Later, one hundred and twenty more received the same Spirit and the heavens were opened for them, and it is still open. However, heaven does not come to earth randomly. When we are anointed by the Holy Spirit we become a gateway to heaven, giving access to angels to come and go and accomplish the will of the Father.

The key here is to walk in the inheritance that Jesus bought for you. You do not have to fight or work for an open heaven over your life, that was already taken care of. The Spirit of God that rests on you is a down payment of heaven on earth. He is from heaven and when He rests on you, heaven is attracted to Him and a connection is established. The things of heaven can now come to earth and the things of earth can be heard in heaven; you become a gate of heaven.

This can not happen through work, fighting, or striving. It happens when you recognize what is going on and cultivate your relationship with the Holy Spirit. We are not fighting for an open heaven, we are fighting from an open heaven. The anointing of the Spirit is the sign that the heavens are already opened, and by growing in our relationship with Him we give God access to the earth around us.

BEING A TEMPLE

[Eph 2:21-22 NKJV] 21 in whom the whole building, being fitted together, grows into a holy temple in the Lord, 22 in whom you also are being built together for a dwelling place of God in the Spirit.

[Eph 5:18-20 NKJV] 18 And do not be drunk with wine, in which is dissipation; but be filled with the Spirit, 19 speaking to one another in psalms and hymns and spiritual songs, singing and making melody in your heart to the Lord, 20 giving thanks always for all things to God the Father in the name of our Lord Jesus Christ

The anointing cannot be hosted alone. Of course much of this chapter is about what we as individuals can do or be to host His presence, but there is a limit to what one person can carry. Only as a corporate body can we be the temple of God, His very dwelling place on earth. By embracing corporate worship we maximize our ability to host Him, and we provide a place for His glory to dwell.

Many have forsaken the gathering together for worship to their own hurt. At some time we started gathering around sermons and doctrine and agreement on issues, and church became very dull. But the people of God are supposed to gather around the presence of God, and that means worship. Extravagant praise, costing us money and time, done with excellence, is what God deserves and loves. A culture in which He is honored and His people are honored is His desire, and He reserves His glory for that alone.

It is time to start going to church for God. It is time to live our lives for God. We know from the scriptures that He loves people and He loves corporate worship, and because we love Him that is what we give. Christianity is not a self-centered, self-help religion. He deserves extravagant worship and that is what He is going to get. Hosting His presence will never be complete without hosting His glory together as His temple on earth.

RELEASING YOUR PEACE

[Mat 10:13 NKJV] 13 "If the household is worthy, let your peace come upon it. But if it is not worthy, let your peace return to you.

[Jhn 14:26-27 NKJV] 26 "But the Helper, the Holy Spirit, whom the Father will send in My name, He will teach you all things, and bring to your remembrance all things that I said to you. 27 "Peace I leave with you, My peace I give to you; not as the world gives do I give to you. Let not your heart be troubled, neither let it be afraid.

All the good things that happen in the kingdom of God - healing, salvation, wholeness, deliverance, restoration - are all the result of the work of the Holy Spirit. We have been given the ability to host Him and to release Him to others. We have talked about what it means to host Him, but how do we purposely release Him to touch the lives of others?

There are some simple yet profound ways to release His presence and power in our lives and the lives of others. One is through touch; whether it is the laying on of hands or a hug given in love, touch can transfer the anointing. Faith is another big one. Words spoken in faith and received by faith transfers the anointing. It could be preaching, prophecy, declarations, prayer or just encouragement, but words spoken in faith and heard in faith releases the Spirit to act. Prophetic acts can also release His presence, as well as extravagant worship. Anointing oil and cloths can carry the presence to those in need. Extreme generosity or acts of sacrificial love releases the anointing. Forgiveness is another important way in which we release Him.

The presence of the Holy Spirit is the presence of peace in our lives. This peace is a tangible state that can be nurtured and released to others. When we are at rest He will rest on us, and when He rests on us we can release that same peace to change other's lives. When we live our lives to host His presence, our senses begin to tune in to how He works and we cooperate with Him to touch the lives of others. It is through the hosting and the transferring of the anointing that everything is done in the kingdom.

LOVE

CHAPTER 7

LOVE IS…

[1Co 13:4-8 NKJV] 4 Love suffers long [and] is kind; love does not envy; love does not parade itself, is not puffed up; 5 does not behave rudely, does not seek its own, is not provoked, thinks no evil; 6 does not rejoice in iniquity, but rejoices in the truth; 7 bears all things, believes all things, hopes all things, endures all things. 8 Love never fails.

LOVE ALWAYS WINS

I love ice cream made from coconut milk. There is a little shop in Pasadena where I had the best thing I have ever put in my mouth, coconut milk ice cream in a coffee caramel flavor that was just amazing. I also love my family, a good cup of coffee, going to the beach, and traveling to new places. When we say that we love something, we mean many different things. We feel enjoyment, compassion, or respect towards something or someone. Perhaps we do not feel much at the moment but we take action to help another, and that is love too. Love is a feeling and an action, and can be focused in many directions.

God created us to feel and do love, to make choices that better those around us. Love can be directed at a pet, a city, or a certain food, and that is perfectly fine. But the love of God goes a step beyond all of that. God's love is more than a feeling or an action, it is an environment. God is love and His presence is the ecosystem in which people were created to thrive in. His love provides the perfect conditions for the human heart to grow and flourish.

Love always wins. When we stay in this place called His love we always prosper, our hearts always grow, and we always reproduce. If you set a young tomato plant out and create the ideal conditions for it, it will never fail to grow. Put it in the perfect soil, water it just enough, give it the right amount of sun and it will always grow. That is how it is created. Put it in the right environment and it will grow bigger, it's roots will go deeper, and tomatoes will hang from it's branches. That is what love does, it creates the environment in which the human soul will never fail to prosper.

GOD IS FOR US

[Rom 8:31-39 NKJV] 31 What then shall we say to these things? If God [is] for us, who [can be] against us? 32 He who did not spare His own Son, but delivered Him up for us all, how shall He not with Him also freely give us all things? 33 Who shall bring a charge against God's elect? [It is] God who justifies. 34 Who [is] he who condemns? [It is] Christ who died, and furthermore is also risen, who is even at the right hand of God, who also makes intercession for us. 35 Who shall separate us from the love of Christ? [Shall] tribulation, or distress, or persecution, or famine, or nakedness, or peril, or sword? 36 As it is written: "For Your sake we are killed all day long; We are accounted as sheep for the slaughter." 37 Yet in all these things we are more than conquerors through Him who loved us. 38 For I am persuaded that neither death nor life, nor angels nor principalities nor powers, nor things present nor things to come, 39 nor height nor depth, nor any other created thing, shall be able to separate us from the love of God which is in Christ Jesus our Lord.

When God created Adam and Eve and put them in the garden, He put them in the perfect environment. Deep communion between God and man, meaningful work, companionship, freedom from fear and anxiety, and continual discovery combined to make a place where they could prosper. It was not a state in which they were controlled or programed to do right, but an atmosphere of grace where they had the dignity to choose right. Satan's goal was to remove them from that place so that he could control them through shame and intimidation. Jesus not only restored that environment, He took it to a whole new level.

Because of Him we can now experience the love of God every day, and flourish in it. But there is more. We are not just restored in relationship to the Father, we are also part of the team that brings restoration to others. Not only is the problem solved, but we are part of the solution! And it gets better; nothing can remove us from this place called the love of God. It does not matter what the enemy does, what circumstances happen, or what any person thinks. We are permanently set in this environment of love and nothing can take us out.

FOR GOD SO LOVED THE WORLD

[Jhn 3:16-17 NKJV] 16 "For God so loved the world that He gave His only begotten Son, that whoever believes in Him should not perish but have everlasting life. 17 "For God did not send His Son into the world to condemn the world, but that the world through Him might be saved.

A religious atmosphere in which every aspect of our lives is controlled is not our natural habitat. Jesus did not come as a judge pronouncing condemnation on us and tightly controlling everything we do. He came as a gift to humanity taking away satan's control and restoring our dignity and ability to choose. Make no mistake, total surrender to God is the only way into the kingdom, but it is not a forced surrender but our choice that He desires.

God so loved the world that He gave us Jesus. That means that He loved us while we were still sinners, and He took the initiative to create an environment in which we could be set free, choose good, and thrive. That is what love does. He did not just love the good people, the church, or Israel. He loved the whole world, every person, and He healed, delivered, taught, forgave, and restored them before they deserved it.

Grace is the atmosphere in which we grow. He gave undeserved mercy and forgiveness, He released revelation that few were seeking, He drove away demons and sickness, and He ultimately sacrificed His life for people chanting to crucify Him. He did not come requiring something that we could not give, He created the environment through His love that brought us to Him. Religion requires from us, love empowers us.

Religion takes a weed-eater to people and then follows with weed killer. It withholds water and nutrients so that the weeds cannot grow. Love freely gives everything that is needed for growth, withholding nothing. It provides us a safe and empowering place to grow. That is what God's love does for us, it gives. It allows us to choose, to mature, and to grow without fear of failure.

FATHER I DESIRE

[Luk 22:15 NKJV] 15 Then He said to them, "With [fervent] desire I have desired to eat this Passover with you before I suffer;

[Jhn 17:24 NKJV] 24 "Father, I desire that they also whom You gave Me may be with Me where I am, that they may behold My glory which You have given Me; for You loved Me before the foundation of the world.

For all of eternity God the Father, God the Son, and God the Holy Spirit exist in this environment called love. Each one being both unique and unified, they fellowship together in never ending communion. In this atmosphere everything flourishes; the trees bear fruit every month, the angels explode with joyous praise, and creativity and prosperity abound. In this place called love, humanity was conceived in the heart of God, and only in this place will we ever be satisfied.

Jesus literally gave His life to create this environment of love for the human race. He deeply cares about us and longingly desires that we share in this fellowship. God's love sent His only Son to us and Jesus's love sacrificed everything to send us the Spirit. Now through the Spirit inside us we can join in the fellowship with God and each other until we grow into an equal partner with Him.

SAFETY

Love looks like many things and has many expressions, but I want to focus on three. God has revealed Himself primarily as a Father and Jesus as a Bridegroom because that is what love looks like. Just like a husband and a father sets the atmosphere of the home, so too God sets an atmosphere of love in which we live. He provides the necessary parameters in which we can live to the fullest. His love provides a place of safety, a sense of enjoyment, and a culture of honor and that is the environment where we grow healthy and whole.

Love is a covering of safety for those who are being loved. It covers a multitude of sins, it believes all things, bears all things, and endures all things. Just like a good father provides for his children, love provides a place of safety for those under it. Love holds off those things that seek to hurt and destroy. It does not require perfection or maturity to get affirmation, but freely gives before we deserve it. Love makes room for the immature, the young, and the weak to grow without fear.

God freely loves us while we are immature, protecting us and gradually increasing our responsibility and freedom when we can handle it. If we are a tender young plant He does not expose us to the harsh elements and then yell at us for failing. He nourishes and cherishes us into maturity and fruitfulness. Love provides undeserved mercy and forgiveness when we need it, desire and power to do right, and the protection and accountability of family. Love makes allowances for weakness and motivation for improvement. Love is an environment of safety that creates optimal growing conditions for all who need it.

ENJOYMENT

When I was a new father and my son was a fussy baby, God spoke to me something I will never forget. It was late one night and He spoke to my heart about my son, "Enjoy him." It was the best relationship advice I have ever read or heard. Those two words changed my whole perspective. People do not thrive when they are ignored, abused, or even tolerated. We are made to be enjoyed by others, and without enjoyment our growth is stunted and our hearts shrivel up.

Love does not just tolerate, it enjoys. It is genuinely happy when the other is there, and smiles at the mere presence of another, not just their performance. Love is an environment in which people are celebrated for who they are, and that is where wholeness is developed. In this place of enjoyment a foundation is laid on which risk and creativity are built and people succeed to new levels of greatness. The place where you cannot fail as long as you try is the place from which great achievements come.

Enjoyment makes the heart come alive. If safety is like the soil we are planted in that provides stability and nourishment for growth, enjoyment is like the water that brings life and joy and motivation for growth. God smiles at our every effort, dances and sings over us, and loves to spend time with us. It is His enjoyment of us and our enjoyment of Him that sparks a long lasting relationship and fruitfulness.

HONOR

Love is a culture in which every person is not only safe and enjoyed, but also honored. In the kingdom or family of God every person is not created equal. Of course we are all loved the same, but we do not all have the same gifts, talents and abilities. God loves diversity and authority, and He creates an environment in which everyone is unique and each person contributes something special to the whole.

The ecosystem of love is one in which every gift from every person is celebrated. People are not meant to conform to a mold, but to uniquely add value to the family through the gifts that are inside them. Honor recognizes the anointing on another's life, it respects the authority of those over it, and it celebrates the gifts of everyone. Love sees through the eyes of honor and does not wait for others to mature, but sees who they are in the future and treats them accordingly.

Safety is the soil, enjoyment is the water, and honor is the sun light. God made the perfect environment for us to flourish, because that is what love does. Love does not just require maturity and greatness, it enables it, providing everything we need to succeed. In this environment called love, we cannot fail.

LOVE

CHAPTER 8

GROWING IN LOVE

[Eph 3:14-19 NKJV] 14 For this reason I bow my knees to the Father of our Lord Jesus Christ, 15 from whom the whole family in heaven and earth is named, 16 that He would grant you, according to the riches of His glory, to be strengthened with might through His Spirit in the inner man, 17 that Christ may dwell in your hearts through faith; that you, being rooted and grounded in love, 18 may be able to comprehend with all the saints what [is] the width and length and depth and height-- 19 to know the love of Christ which passes knowledge; that you may be filled with all the fullness of God.

ALL FRUITFULNESS COMES FROM INTIMACY

[Jhn 15:4 NKJV] 4 "Abide in Me, and I in you. As the branch cannot bear fruit of itself, unless it abides in the vine, neither can you, unless you abide in Me.

[Eph 2:13 NKJV] 13 But now in Christ Jesus you who once were far off have been brought near by the blood of Christ.

Because of what Jesus has done for us we have been brought near, into a position of closeness to the heart of God. We now relate to God the way a wife relates to her husband. As the bride of Christ we have His ear and we get to know His thoughts and desires. Enjoying each other's presence, talking and listening to each other, doing things together, and learning about each other's hearts is how we are meant to relate to God.

Every good thing, every breakthrough, every heart changed, and every miracle come from heaven through Jesus to earth. There is literally nothing of any lasting importance that happens that does not originate in Him. In the same way that a wife cannot bear a child without her husband, or a branch cannot bear any fruit without the vine, so too we cannot bear any fruit without Him. Only through intimacy with Jesus does your life produce anything. Without a real and deep one on one relationship with Him there is nothing good growing in you. As Heidi Baker says and demonstrates so well, "all fruitfulness comes from intimacy."

But not all intimacy is for fruitfulness. We are not just a fruit factory, only engaging with the heart of God so that we can produce fruit. As the companions of Jesus, we enjoy Him and He enjoys us just for the fun of it. Take time to both talk to Him and listen to Him. Sing together, work together, be quiet together and just love Him. Worship with genuine gratefulness in your heart, listen with genuine intention of believing what He says, and allow Him the joy of knowing your real hopes and dreams.

JESUS' LOVE LANGUAGE

[Jhn 14:21 NKJV] 21 "He who has My commandments and keeps them, it is he who loves Me. And he who loves Me will be loved by My Father, and I will love him and manifest Myself to him."

Did you know that Jesus has a love language? You may have read the book about the five love languages, how people give and receive love in different ways. If you know how someone else desires to receive love, then you can more effectively show them your affection. Jesus' love language is obedience! Not just mindless obedience to a set of rules, but loving obedience to every word He speaks. If you want to make Jesus really happy, this is how you do it. You stay close to Him and listen carefully to every word He says, then you quickly obey with all your heart.

This chapter is about how we take whatever love we have and increase it. There are several keys to that happening in our lives, but this idea in John 14 could be the most important. God is love and all love comes from Him, so in order to increase in love we have to allow Him to manifest Himself through us. Jesus loves when we attentively obey the promptings He gives us, and He promises to manifest Himself in our lives when we do.

So in order to grow in love we follow this cycle of lovingly getting to know the heart of Jesus, listening to His promptings, and quickly believing and obeying His words. Every time we do that He manifests His presence and good things happen. Our hearts grow in their capacity to love and then we do it all again. This is how we continually grow in the love of God.

THAT I MIGHT KNOW HIM

[Phl 1:9 NKJV] 9 And this I pray, that your love may abound still more and more in knowledge and all discernment

[Phl 3:8-10 NKJV] 8 Yet indeed I also count all things loss for the excellence of the knowledge of Christ Jesus my Lord, for whom I have suffered the loss of all things, and count them as rubbish, that I may gain Christ 9 and be found in Him, not having my own righteousness, which [is] from the law, but that which [is] through faith in Christ, the righteousness which is from God by faith; 10 that I may know Him and the power of His resurrection, and the fellowship of His sufferings, being conformed to His death

Growing in love goes hand in hand with growing in knowledge. Not the knowledge of facts and figures, but the knowledge of the Son of God. Love is not a thing, a feeling, a set of actions, or a decision. Love is a person named Jesus. Love has thoughts, dreams desires, and plans. He likes certain things and does not like other things. He is inherently good, therefore when we get to know Him more we are at the same time growing in Love.

Just like any other relationship, it takes time to get to know someone. As we spend time with Jesus we get to know Him. We find out the things He is passionate about, and the things He hates. We feel His touch and experience His presence. His voice becomes clearer and His dreams become our dreams. This is growing in love, growing in our intimate knowledge of who He is.

To know Him is to love Him. The more we get to know Him the bigger our hearts get and the more we love. He makes us feel safe, enjoyed, and honored like we talked about last chapter. The things that hinder love like guilt, shame, doubt, and bitterness are washed away as His heart expands in us. We enjoy His presence more and more, long for His approval, come to Him when we make mistakes, and become more and more like Him.

Love for God, for ourselves, and for others grows at the same rate. There is no such thing as loving God and not loving people. Love is love. The more we get to know Him the more we love to worship, the more we take care of ourselves, and the more compassion we have for others. We do not have to prioritize a list of who to love, putting ourselves last, and go through some self-help process to love more. We simply have to grow in our relationship with Jesus and let his love shine through in every area of our lives.

FREELY RECEIVE, FREELY GIVE

[Mat 10:8 NKJV] 8 "Heal the sick, cleanse the lepers, raise the dead, cast out demons. Freely you have received, freely give.

Everything in the kingdom of God, including love, is increased by good stewardship. We are the sons and daughters of God, not just His slaves. We do not work to please Him, He is already pleased with us. He does not just pay us wages in exchange for our time and effort, He has made us a part of the family business of bringing wholeness to people and the planet.

That means that we have to be good receivers in order to be good givers. In order to grow the family business, the son has to freely accept the inheritance that the father worked for and then build on top of that. Many people walk around like orphans unable to receive from God what is already bought and paid for because they feel like they have to earn it. When that happens there ends up being a whole bunch of baby Christians who barely make any progress in life because they are just trying to survive. But that is not the way of the kingdom nor the intention of God.

In the same way that Jesus called the disciples who had done nothing to deserve Him and freely gave them all things, He does the same for us. He freely gives us forgiveness, healing, deliverance, peace, joy, love, gifts and so on and then expects us to grow and mature in those things and freely give to others. They in turn freely receive and freely give and the business expands. If every person and every generation starts from scratch, feeling like they have to earn their own way, then progress is very minimal. But if each of us freely receives what God and others have already worked for, then our efforts will contribute to real growth in the kingdom.

This is what love looks like. God initiated love by freely giving us Jesus. Jesus freely received the affirmation of the Father, the anointing of the Spirit, and favor with people. He then increased it to a whole new level by laying His life down for us. He freely gave to the disciples and then expected them to grow in love and freely give it to others. We now have available to us not only what Jesus did for us, but every breakthrough that has come since. When we honor those who have gone before us, we receive what they fought for, take it, increase it and give it to the next generation.

LOVE

CHAPTER 9

THE GREENHOUSE EFFECT

[Isa 58:10-12 NKJV] 10 [If] you extend your soul to the hungry And satisfy the afflicted soul, Then your light shall dawn in the darkness, And your darkness shall [be] as the noonday. 11 The LORD will guide you continually, And satisfy your soul in drought, And strengthen your bones; You shall be like a watered garden, And like a spring of water, whose waters do not fail. 12 Those from among you Shall build the old waste places; You shall raise up the foundations of many generations; And you shall be called the Repairer of the Breach, The Restorer of Streets to Dwell In.

[Isa 61:1-4 NKJV] 1 "The Spirit of the Lord GOD [is] upon Me, Because the LORD has anointed Me To preach good tidings to the poor; He has sent Me to heal the brokenhearted, To proclaim liberty to the captives, And the opening of the prison to [those who are] bound; 2 To proclaim the acceptable year of the LORD, And the day of vengeance of our God; To comfort all who mourn, 3 To console those who mourn in Zion, To give them beauty for ashes, The oil of joy for mourning, The garment of praise for the spirit of heaviness; That they may be called trees of righteousness, The planting of the LORD, that He may be glorified." 4 And they shall rebuild the old ruins, They shall raise up the former desolations, And they shall repair the ruined cities, The desolations of many generations.

[Jer 31:12 NKJV] 12 Therefore they shall come and sing in the height of Zion, Streaming to the goodness of the LORD--For wheat and new wine and oil, For the young of the flock and the herd; Their souls shall be like a well-watered garden, And they shall sorrow no more at all.

A WELL-WATERED GARDEN

Love provides the optimal conditions in which the word and the anointing of God works in our lives to produce maximum growth and fruitfulness. The Father not only creates those conditions for us, He desires to partner with us to create those conditions for others. We have discussed what love is and does, and we have studied how to grow in love. Now let us discover how to partner with the God of love in ministry to others.

As we read in the scriptures above, when we say yes to love we are saying yes to the very heart of God. It creates a connection between ourselves and the mighty river of God from which we drink and become satisfied. But the river does not stop when we are satisfied, it keeps flowing until our lives are a well-watered garden that others can drink from. The more we say yes to love and drink of that river, the larger our garden becomes and the more people can drink from our lives.

When we love well, our sphere of influence becomes like a greenhouse. In the same way a greenhouse is used to create perfect growing conditions for plants, love creates perfect growing conditions for those around us. The farmer builds a greenhouse for many reasons. With it he can provide safety to his plants from frost and storms and pests. The greenhouse extends his growing season so that fruit can be produced year round. He can install the best soil, plant the best seeds, remove the weeds quickly, and provide optimal moisture and temperature.

As we allow God to not only love us but also love through us, we are building a greenhouse for those around us. Love protects and cherishes them, plants only the words of God, waters with the anointing of the Spirit, and raises up good and noble hearts that receive those words, grow, and multiply. This is what Jesus did for us and what He is sending us to do for others. Not just preaching the word or moving in the anointing, but also creating a safe place for maximum growth.

PROVIDING SAFETY

[Mat 9:35-38 NKJV] 35 Then Jesus went about all the cities and villages, teaching in their synagogues, preaching the gospel of the kingdom, and healing every sickness and every disease among the people. 36 But when He saw the multitudes, He was moved with compassion for them, because they were weary and scattered, like sheep having no shepherd. 37 Then He said to His disciples, "The harvest truly [is] plentiful, but the laborers [are] few. 38 "Therefore pray the Lord of the harvest to send out laborers into His harvest."

Jesus was and is a powerhouse of the anointing, more anointed than anyone ever. He is also the Word of God, and when He speaks it is life to those who hear. But He is more than that. He is the Good Shepherd of the sheep, moved with compassion for us and providing a safe place for us to grow. He is love, and it showed in every interaction He had with people.

Of course He moved in the gifts of the Spirit, giving revelation that was mind blowing. But it was not about just saying the word of knowledge or prophecy, He said it in a way that they could hear. He protected those who did not yet believe by making His teaching only for those who were ready to receive it. He was easy to talk to, and average people felt safe with Him.

This is especially evident by the amount of faith He required to release a miracle. He knew that it took both the anointing and faith to release miracles, but He did not put the burden on others. He cultivated the anointing so much in His life that very little faith was required from others. Often He said that only a mustard seed of faith would be enough to produce a great miracle, because He hosted the presence to the point that just a little faith would work. Instead of demanding of people what they did not have to give, He would give them something to do or say that would activate their faith so that He could bless them.

Jesus took on the role of protector of people, not accuser. Remember the picture of love that He painted in the story of the good Samaritan? Love looked like providing a safe place for the other to recover and did not require anything from him. Jesus demonstrated that when He defeated satan in the wilderness and again on the cross. He did not blame people for being oppressed by demons. He took the initiative, defeated the enemy, and delivered the people. He became an umbrella of safety for others to encounter God without fear.

This is what we are called to do. Ministry is about providing an environment in which people do not just hear the word, they receive it. We build a shelter of anointing in which others can come and freely encounter God before they deserve it. Just like a father creates a safe environment for his children, so we do for others. We make it easy for others to thrive because they are under our protection.

PROVIDING ENJOYMENT

[Jhn 13:1 NKJV] 1 Now before the Feast of the Passover, when Jesus knew that His hour had come that He should depart from this world to the Father, having loved His own who were in the world, He loved them to the end.

[Jhn 14:3, 18 NKJV] 3 "And if I go and prepare a place for you, I will come again and receive you to Myself; that where I am, [there] you may be also. ... 18 "I will not leave you orphans; I will come to you.

[Jhn 15:11-12, 15, 17 NKJV] 11 "These things I have spoken to you, that My joy may remain in you, and [that] your joy may be full. 12 "This is My commandment, that you love one another as I have loved you. ... 15 "No longer do I call you servants, for a servant does not know what his master is doing; but I have called you friends, for all things that I heard from My Father I have made known to you. ... 17 "These things I command you, that you love one another.

[Jhn 16:22, 24, 27, 33 NKJV] 22 "Therefore you now have sorrow; but I will see you again and your heart will rejoice, and your joy no one will take from you. ... 24 "Until now you have asked nothing in My name. Ask, and you will receive, that your joy may be full. ... 27 "for the Father Himself loves you, because you have loved Me, and have believed that I came forth from God. ... 33 "These things I have spoken to you, that in Me you may have peace. In the world you will have tribulation; but be of good cheer, I have overcome the world."

[Jhn 17:13, 18, 21-24 NKJV] 13 "But now I come to You, and these things I speak in the world, that they may have My joy fulfilled in themselves. ... 18 "As You sent Me into the world, I also have sent them into the world. ... 21 "that they all may be one, as You, Father, [are] in Me, and I in You; that they also may be one in Us, that the world may believe that You sent Me. 22 "And the glory which You gave Me I have given them, that they may be one just as We are one: 23 "I in them, and You in Me; that they may be made perfect in one, and that the world may know that You have sent Me, and have loved them as You have loved Me. 24 "Father, I desire that they also whom You gave Me may be with Me where I am, that they may behold My glory which You have given Me; for You loved Me before the foundation of the world.

In John 13-17 we really get a sense of the heart of Jesus. He really loved those guys, and it showed not just in His sacrifice for them but also in His enjoyment of them. It is really hard to make a case that you love someone if you are not glad to see them when they come around you. Love is more than just providing for them and keeping them safe. Love is happiness that they are with you. Love is liking someone for who they are. Love is laughing with them, working with them, and playing with them.

Love is enjoyment. People long to be enjoyed by another, and we are called to provide that for them. The human heart thrives when it is enjoyed, not when it is tolerated. You can preach the best sermons, teach the greatest truth, and move in the power of God. But the best seeds still do not grow in hard hearts, and if you dump a bucket of water on hard soil most of it just runs off and is wasted. Love cares about the condition of the heart, not just the seeds and water.

Jesus took the time and attention to enjoy people, care about them, and celebrate who they were. He ate with them, listened to them, and lived with them. It showed because people, not just the cool people but even the broken, liked to be around Him. People like you when you like them, and Jesus liked people and they knew it. His love softened their hearts to receive the word and the anointing. Love looks like caring about the conditions of the hearts around us, not blaming them for their hardness, but providing the enjoyment that will soften them up.

We can only enjoy others at this level if we feel Him enjoying us. Remember that it is the same river that we drink from that flows through us and turns our life into a well-watered garden. When we become this garden in which others are celebrated and set free, then and only then will they be able to rebuild their families and communities and cities.

PROVIDING HONOR

[Mat 10:5-8 NKJV] 5 These twelve Jesus sent out and commanded them, saying: "Do not go into the way of the Gentiles, and do not enter a city of the Samaritans. 6 "But go rather to the lost sheep of the house of Israel. 7 "And as you go, preach, saying, 'The kingdom of heaven is at hand.' 8 "Heal the sick, cleanse the lepers, raise the dead, cast out demons. Freely you have received, freely give.

[Luk 10:1, 17 NKJV] 1 After these things the Lord appointed seventy others also, and sent them two by two before His face into every city and place where He Himself was about to go. ... 17 Then the seventy returned with joy, saying, "Lord, even the demons are subject to us in Your name."

Love is a place where the immature can develop. When Jesus called the disciples it was not because of their maturity or giftedness, but He saw something inside them that they did not even see themselves. He chose them, He supplied the anointing,

He taught them the word, He called them into greatness, and He loved them until they matured into who they were supposed to be. Love does not just require maturity, it enables it.

Love sees the seed of greatness in another and honors what the Lord is doing in their life. It creates the environment for them to succeed by allowing them a safe place to try and fail without rejection. When we love others while they are still less than perfect, we give them the grace they need to move forward. Love sets people up for success by designing a culture that honors taking risks and empowers the weak.

Jesus called the disciples while they were ordinary men, with no requirements except to follow Him. He taught them, demonstrated the kingdom for them, and empowered them. As they recognized who He was they honored Him as a great teacher, miracle worker, and eventually as the Son of God. The honor that they gave Him allowed them to access the anointing on His life, because one of the ways the anointing is transferred is through honor. Now they are doing miracles themselves, not because of their own relationship with the Father, but because of His.

This culture of honor that they developed in which Jesus honored them even in their immaturity and they honored Him as their father created an atmosphere for success. They were able to do what Jesus did because they honored Him, and Jesus was able to love them in spite of their mistakes because He honored them. Love does not parade itself around as the only answer to the world's problems, but it builds a family culture of honor that reproduces itself in others.

The anointed man or woman of God is not an island of insecurity and self-promotion. Just being able to move in the gifts of the Spirit is not enough. Faith by itself will stay by itself, but when you take great faith and great anointing and mix it with great love, you build that greenhouse where others can follow in your footsteps and hopefully pass you up. Love builds that culture of honor that allows people to operate in an atmosphere of God's presence and the anointing that they did not work for until they are mature enough to have their own.

BECOMING FATHERS AND MOTHERS

[1Th 2:7-8, 11-12 NKJV] 7 But we were gentle among you, just as a nursing [mother] cherishes her own children. 8 So, affectionately longing for you, we were well pleased to impart to you not only the gospel of God, but also our own lives, because you had become dear to us. ... 11 as you know how we exhorted, and comforted, and charged every one of you, as a father [does] his own children, 12 that you would walk worthy of God who calls you into His own kingdom and glory.

[Rom 1:11 NKJV] 11 For I long to see you, that I may impart to you some spiritual gift, so that you may be established

[Eph 4:11-15 NKJV] 11 And He Himself gave some [to be] apostles, some prophets, some evangelists, and some pastors and teachers, 12 for the equipping of the saints for the work of ministry, for the edifying of the body of Christ, 13 till we all come to the unity of the faith and of the knowledge of the Son of God, to a perfect man, to the measure of the stature of the fullness of Christ; 14 that we should no longer be children, tossed to and fro and carried about with every wind of doctrine, by the trickery of men, in the cunning craftiness of deceitful plotting, 15 but, speaking the truth in love, may grow up in all things into Him who is the head--Christ

As we grow in faith, the anointing, and love, Jesus is going to arrest our hearts for our cities, regions, and nations. He is calling us to become more than just believers, but fathers and mothers in the kingdom. Love demands it. Fathers and mothers do what no one else can do. They do not live unto themselves, but partner with the heart of God to see others come into their destiny.

The apostle Paul was a great example of this. He brought the message of the gospel to those who did not deserve it. He healed the sick, cast out the demons, and taught the people. He labored in prayer for them, nurtured and cherished them, and never required anything from them. He earned their honor and respect and then used that honor to release others into the ministry. Challenging them to be like Christ, he gave them an example to follow.

This is what love does, it turns us into fathers and mothers. Fathers impart gifts to others and then teach them how to use it. They equip others to do the work of the ministry. They work hard to build up an inheritance and then give it away for free so that their sons and daughters can build on the foundation they laid and not have to start over.

Love sends us to build an ecosystem in which many others will flourish. That is what God did for us and it is what He is calling us to do for Him. Love, given enough time, produces wholeness in those around us and whole people are powerful people. Whole people do not have shame, guilt, doubt, anxiety and fear blocking the flow of God in their lives. They are rich in faith, covered in the anointing, and full of love. We are called to be powerful people who produce powerful people who rebuild the cities and regions of the world.

[Eph 3:14-19 NKJV] 14 For this reason I bow my knees to the Father of our Lord Jesus Christ, 15 from whom the whole family in heaven and earth is named, 16 that He would grant you, according to the riches of His glory, to be strengthened with might through His Spirit in the inner man, 17 that Christ may dwell in your hearts through faith; that you, being rooted and grounded in love, 18 may be able to comprehend with all the saints what [is] the width and length and depth and height-- 19 to know the love of Christ which passes knowledge; that you may be filled with all the fullness of God.

ABOUT THE AUTHOR

John Bradbury lives in east Tennessee with his wife Shannon and their five children. Previously on staff at the International House of Prayer in Kansas City for seven years, they are currently contending for revival in their region. John is passionate about hearing the voice of God, healing, and equipping others for ministry. He enjoys long hours in the presence of God, being outdoors, Crossfit, and family. This is his first book.

.

65564138R00080

Made in the USA
Lexington, KY
16 July 2017